GLOBAL FINANCIAL MARKETS AND THE UK BANKING INDUSTRY

Activity 1 | Key terms

Select the correct key term from the list below to match each definition:

a Government bond		**b** Insurance		**c** Investment bank	
d Systemic risk		**e** Crowding out		**f** G20	
g Interest rate		**h** Banks' capital ratio		**i** Liquidity	
j Moral hazard					

1	The possibility that an event at the company level could trigger severe instability or collapse an entire industry or economy	
2	When an individual or organisation takes many more risks than they should do because they know that they are either covered by insurance, or that the government will protect them from any damage incurred	
3	An arrangement by which a company or the state undertakes to provide a guarantee of compensation for specified loss, damage, illness, or death in return for payment of a specified premium	
4	An informal group of 19 countries and the European Union, with representatives of the International Monetary Fund and the World Bank	
5	The cost of borrowing and the reward for saving	
6	An IOU that the government issues in return for money to fund its spending plans	
7	A situation when increased government bond interest rates lead to a reduction in private investment spending such that it dampens the initial increase of total investment spending	
8	The ease and cost with which assets can be turned into cash and used immediately as a means of exchange	
9	A firm which will underwrite new debt and equity securities for all types of corporations, aid in the sale of securities, and help to facilitate mergers and acquisitions, reorganizations and broker trades for both institutions and private investors	
10	The relationship between the funds a bank has in reserve against the riskier assets it holds that could be vulnerable in the event of a crisis	

Activity 2 | How do interest rates work in UK financial markets?

The Bank of England (BoE) is the Central Bank of the UK.

Question 1
....

Does the Bank of England aim to make a profit? Explain your answer.

Question 2
....

Which type of macroeconomic policy is the BoE responsible for, in order to help the government to achieve its macroeconomic objectives?

One of the BoE's roles is to set the 'BASE RATE' of interest – aka 'BANK RATE' – and to review it each month. The Bank's website says: 'We set Bank Rate to influence other interest rates. We use our influence to keep inflation low and stable.'

Question 3
....

Which body is responsible for setting the Base Rate?

Banks and building societies operating in the UK hold reserve accounts at the Bank of England – these are effectively instant-access accounts for financial firms that participate in the UK – known as the 'Sterling Monetary Framework'. The BoE pays interest at Base Rate on these reserves.

Question 4
....

What is the current UK Base Rate?

Question 5
....

Find out what rate of interest you could get today if you opened an instant access savings account at one of the major high-street banks.

Reserve balances can be varied freely to meet day-to-day liquidity needs, for example to accommodate unexpected payment flows.

Whenever payments are made between customers at different banks, they are ultimately settled by transferring money held at the BoE (reserves) between the reserves accounts of those banks.

Because the amount of money a bank has available fluctuates daily, based on its lending activities and its customers' withdrawal and deposit activity, the bank may experience a shortage or surplus of cash at the end of the business day.

Question 6

What is the term used when individuals experience a shortage of cash at the end of the day in their instant access bank account?

Those who have a surplus can leave their money as reserves at the BoE and gain the Base Rate of interest on it.

Those who have a shortage need to borrow on a very short-term basis – known as 'overnight lending'. They can borrow it from the BoE – or from others who have an overnight surplus.

Those banks that experience a surplus often lend money overnight to banks that experience a shortage, so the banking system remains stable and liquid.

This means that overnight market rates between the banks stay close to the official Bank Rate, as there is no incentive for banks to borrow from or lend to each other at rates much different from Bank Rate.

However, when banks lend to customers, they need to make a profit over the rate at which they can borrow, so at this point they start to add a higher interest rate. That rate will vary depend on:

- the risk they feel they are taking by lending to that borrower (higher risk = higher interest)
- the level of competition between them and other potential lenders – ie substitute suppliers of lending
- the PED of the borrower – more inelastic PED = higher interest rate can be charged

Therefore, rates available to customers who borrow or save will be above the Base Rate.

Question 7

Carry out some research to find out what interest rates are now and have been for the last 10 years for:

a A £10,000 unsecured loan

b A two-year fixed rate mortgage on a 75% loan-to-value mortgage

c A two-year fixed rate mortgage on a 90% loan-to-value mortgage

Activity 3 | What are financial markets?

A financial market is any exchange that facilitates the trading of financial instruments, such as stocks, bonds, foreign exchange, or primary commodities such as oil and gas.

There are three main categories of financial market:

| 1 | The money market | 2 | The capital market | 3 | The foreign exchange market |

The table below has 12 features of financial markets, but four of them apply to each of these three markets. Sort the features to match the three different markets.

These are the markets where securities such as shares, and bonds are issued to raise medium to long-term financing	Includes short term government borrowing e.g. 3-12 months Treasury Bills – to help fund the government's budget (fiscal) deficit	Includes raising of finance by the government through the issue/sale of medium-term - long term government bonds for example 10 year and 20-year bonds (loans)
Money is borrowed and lent normally for up to 12 months	The average value of trade per day is $7.5trillion in 2022	The spot rate is the price of a currency to be delivered now, and the forward rate is a fixed price given for buying a currency today to be delivered in the future
Huge gains or losses are made by traders– speculative activity in the market is often high	Market for medium-longer term loan finance	On average, there were around 11.1 billion trades every day on the US market in 2022

Includes inter-bank lending i.e. the commercial banks providing liquidity for each other	A market where currencies (foreign exchange) are traded. There is no single currency market – it is made up of the thousands of trading floors	Market for short term loan finance for businesses and households

The money market:

1

2

3

4

Capital market:

1

2

3

4

Foreign exchange market:

1

2

3

4

Activity 4 | Global financial centres

The Global Financial Centre Index provides a way of ranking the competitiveness of financial cities/centres around the world. The index is constructed via a mix of questionnaires as well as metrics from a number of other sources, including the OECD and World Bank. It is published twice each year.

The index includes aspects such as:

Human Capital	Business environment	Infrastructure	Financial sector development	Reputation
• Level of appropriate skill • Quality of business education • Labour force flexibility • Quality of life	• Level of regulation • Level of taxes • Level of corruption • Economic freedom • Ease of "doing business"	• Availability of transport • Price / availability of office space • Speed of internet	• Volume & value of trading in capital markets • Cluster effects / external economies of scale in finance • Employment and economic growth	• Innovation • Diversity • Brand appeal

This table shows the Top 20 global financial centres in 2009 and 2022. Study the table and then answer the questions that follow.

Top financial centres in 2022		Top financial centres in 2009	
1 New York	11 Paris	1 London	11 Sydney
2 London	12 Seoul	2 New York	12 Frankfurt
3 Hong Kong	13 Chicago	3 Hong Kong	13 Toronto
4 Shanghai	14 Boston	4 Singapore	14 Jersey
5 Los Angeles	15 Washington, D.C.	5 Shenzhen	15 Guernsey
6 Mumbai	16 Frankfurt	6 Zurich	16 Luxembourg
7 Singapore	17 Dubai	7 Tokyo	17 San Francisco
8 Beijing	18 Madrid	8 Chicago	18 Boston
9 Tokyo	19 Amsterdam	9 Geneva	19 Paris
10 Shenzhen	20 Zurich	10 Shanghai	20 Washington

Question 1

Describe the main changes in the rankings of global financial markets over the period shown.

Question 2

Identify and explain reasons why these changes might have occurred.

Question 3

Read this report from Long Finance (the organisation behind the index) on how this data might change over coming years and summarise the key features.

Question 4

Carry out your own research to complete the table below relating to the world's largest Stock Exchanges (by market capitalisation).

Rank	Name of Stock Exchange and location	Market capitalisation	Number of companies listed	Examples of 3 well-known companies listed on this exchange
1				
2				
3				

Table continued on next page.

Rank	Name of Stock Exchange and location	Market capitalisation	Number of companies listed	Examples of 3 well-known companies listed on this exchange
4				
5				
6				
7				
8				
9				
10				

Activity 5 | UK Prudential Regulation – True or False?

Download this description of the work of the Prudential Regulation Authority in the UK, and follow some of the links in it for further information about stress testing, the FPC and insurance companies. Use this research to decide whether each of the following statements is True or False.

		True or False
1	The economy is only healthy if people have confidence in financial institutions, markets and infrastructure	
2	When a consumer buys a policy with an insurer, they should be able to expect it to pay out when they need it.	
3	The role of the PRA is to ensure that firms act safely and raise the chance of getting into financial difficulty	
4	The PRA was established as part of the response to lack of confidence in financial services after the financial crisis of 2007	
5	As part of its supervision of banks, building societies, credit unions, insurance companies and major investment firms, the PRA sets the level of interest that they are allowed to charge	

	True or False
6 Tailored supervision by the PRA ensures that procedures which work well at one bank or financial institution are put in place in others as well	
7 'Stress testing' is used by the financial industry to help gauge investment risk and the adequacy of assets, but not to evaluate an institution's internal processes and controls.	
8 The PRA and the FCA did not replace the old FSA until 2013	
9 Both the PRA and the FCA are involved in improving consumer protection	
10 The PRA scrutinises the stability of individual financial businesses; this is micro-prudential regulation	
11 The FPC identifies, monitors and takes action to remove or reduce systemic risks with a view to protecting and enhancing the resilience of the global financial system; this is macro-prudential regulation	
12 Insurance companies use customers' premiums to invest in companies, stocks and bonds	

Activity 6 | Global financial stability

Watch the video about the work of the Financial Stability Board of the G20.

Take brief notes about how the FSB has attempted to make the global financial system safer, simpler and fairer than it was before the 2007-08 financial crisis, using the following headings:

1 The global financial crisis of 2007-08 and the cost of supporting banking sectors.

2 What is the aim of the reforms of the FSB?

3 Changes for a safer banking system.

a Capital requirements

b Shadow banking

4 Changes for a simple financial system.

a Derivatives

b Hub and spoke model

5 Changes for a fairer financial system.

a The old system – too big to fail

b New system – who foots the bill for failure?

6 Bankers' pay – new international standards.

7 Forward looking controls

Activity 7 | The IMF Global Financial Stability Report

Search online to find the most recent edition of the International Monetary Fund's Global Financial Stability Report.

Question 1
....
Open a link to the Executive Summary of the report, and find three key issues that have been identified and three key pieces of advice to policymakers.

Question 2
....
Suggest which individuals or bodies would be responsible for implementing those pieces of advice in the UK financial markets.

GLOBAL TRADE FLOWS AND PATTERNS

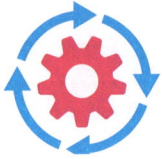

Activity 1 | Definitions

Match each of these terms with one of the definitions given below:

a	Supply chain	**b**	Trade creation	**c**	Comparative advantage
d	Quota	**e**	Terms of trade	**f**	Emerging economy
g	Protectionism	**h**	Logistics	**i**	Trade diversion
j	Trading bloc				

1	The relative advantage that one country or producer has over another
2	A switch from a lower-cost foreign source/supplier outside of a customs union towards a higher-cost supplier located inside the customs union
3	The real value of countries exports in terms of their imports. Also knows as the 'real exchange rate'
4	The management of the flow of goods between the point of origin and the point of consumption to meet requirements of customers or corporations
5	A group of countries co-operating to liberalise trade between each other
6	A network between a company and its suppliers to produce and distribute a specific product to the final buyer
7	Tariff and non-tariff restrictions on imports to protect domestic producers
8	The movement from a higher cost source of output to a lower cost source of supply as a result of joining a trade agreement
9	Typically, a lower to middle income country that is progressing toward becoming more advanced, usually by means of rapid growth, urbanisation and industrialisation
10	A trade barrier that imposes a physical limit on the quantity of a good that can be imported into a country in a given period of time

Activity 2 | Measuring global trade

DHL

DHL is one of the world's largest logistics businesses, and their role in worldwide transport and delivery of goods makes them an 'enabler of global trade'. They do business in over 220 countries and are one of the top ten largest employers in the world.

One result is that they are in a great position to measure changes in the volume and pattern of global trade. They use this data to produce an index of changes in trade, on a global basis and also for individual countries, which is published online four times a year.

Question 1

What are the key factors which drive an increase in global trade?

DHL GLOBAL TRADE BAROMETER
A NEW AND UNIQUE LEADING INDICATOR FOR THE WORLD ECONOMY
BASED ON TRADE OF INTERMEDIATES AND EARLY-CYCLE GOODS

IMPORT AND EXPORT DATA **FROM 7 COUNTRIES**

240 MILLION VARIABLES EVALUATED

REPRESENTING **75 % OF GLOBAL TRADE**

3-MONTH OUTLOOK FOR GLOBAL TRADE

10 INDUSTRIES FROM CHEMICALS TO VEHICLES

UPDATED 4 TIMES A YEAR

#DHL_gtb   logisticsofthings.dhl/gtb   _DHL_

On the web, find the most recent edition of the DHL Global Trade Barometer.

Question 2

On a global scale, has trade increased or decreased since the last report?

Question 3

What is the trend over the last year, and the last five years?

Question 4

Is there a different pattern for air transport and for ocean transport?

Question 5

What is given as the main reason (reasons) for the most recent changes?

Open and read the Country Specific reports for the UK, and at least one other country.

Question 6

For each country, has trade increased or decreased since the last report?

Question 7

What is the trend over the last year, and the last five years?

Question 8

What is the pattern for imports and for exports, and for what kinds of goods, for each country?

Question 9

Which is the more significant factor determining the change in the volume of trade : changes in imports or changes in exports?

Question 10

Is there a different pattern for air transport and for ocean transport?

Activity 3 | Terms of Trade

Visit this part of the OECD website to find data on the Terms of Trade for key OECD countries: and then answer the questions that follow.

Question 1

What is the Terms of Trade ratio, and how is it calculated?

Question 2

What does it mean if a country has an improving Terms of Trade ratio?

Question 3

Which countries shown have an improving Terms of Trade ratio?

Question 4

Is the UK's Terms of Trade ratio improving or worsening, and what are the implications of this for the UK economy?

Activity 4 | UK patterns of trade

Each year the ONS publishes the 'Pink Book' which contains data about the previous year's international trade. The 2022 Pink Book can be found here:

Find the most recent edition of the Pink Book and scan to find the interactive tool that shows the UK's trade in goods with the rest of the world.

It is likely to look like this:

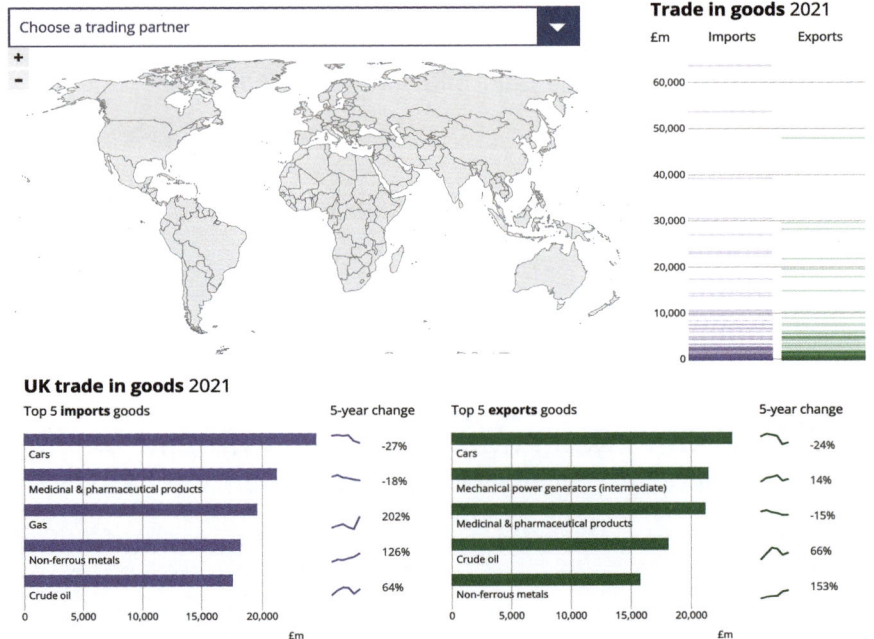

Choose a trading partner

Trade in goods 2021

£m   Imports   Exports

60,000

50,000

40,000

30,000

20,000

10,000

0

UK trade in goods 2021

Top 5 **imports** goods	5-year change
Cars	-27%
Medicinal & pharmaceutical products	-18%
Gas	202%
Non-ferrous metals	126%
Crude oil	64%

0   5,000   10,000   15,000   20,000   £m

Top 5 **exports** goods	5-year change
Cars	-24%
Mechanical power generators (intermediate)	14%
Medicinal & pharmaceutical products	-15%
Crude oil	66%
Non-ferrous metals	153%

0   5,000   10,000   15,000   20,000   £m

Question 1

Record the UK's top 5 imports in goods and top 5 exports in goods, and note the percentage change in each of them over the last five years.

What does the pattern of change suggest?

Question 2

On the ONS Pink Book website, scroll down from the above chart to find the equivalent chart for UK Trade in Services. Record the UK's top 5 imports in services and top 5 exports in services, and note the extent of surplus on this account.

Activity 5 | Multinational companies

Over 25% of Britain's GDP is produced by foreign owned companies. Some of the best-known examples include BAA, owners of most of the UK's airports including Heathrow, now owned by Spanish company Grupo Ferrioval, Cadbury's which is owned by US giant Mondelez and even Boots the Chemist is owned by US retail giant Wal-Mart.

Question 1

3 way match up. Match the logo with the company and country of origin.

Logo	Company	Country
Shell	Home Entertainment, technology	Germany
P&G	Banking	Japan
Honda	Restaurant chain	Brazil
Santander	Footwear	Italy
Michelin	Aviation	Anglo/ Dutch
Nando's	Car manufacture	South Korea
havaianas	Luxury fashion	USA
LG	Oil and gas	South Africa
Lufthansa	Car tyres	Spain
Gucci	Food and toiletries manufacture	France

Question 2

1 **Which of the following is a type of economy of scale?**

A Transfer pricing ☐

B Lower costs of factor inputs ☐

C Diminishing returns ☐

D Marketing economies of scale ☐

2 **Samsung locates a television manufacturing plant in Thailand. Which of the following will most likely benefit the host country?**

A Monopoly power ☐

B Structural unemployment ☐

C External economies of scale in television manufacturing ☐

D Local multiplier effects ☐

3 **Which of the following best explains one reason for the growth in multinational companies:**

A Global divergence of consumer tastes ☐

B Higher levels of trade protection ☐

C Growth in information channels facilitated by the internet ☐

D Exchange controls ☐

4 **Multinational companies can achieve higher profits through:**

A Marginal cost pricing ☐

B Risk bearing economies ☐

C Tax avoidance ☐

D Local multiplier effects ☐

5 **A multinational shoe manufacturer decides to leave a country which had been a major exporter of shoes. This will lead to:**

A Marginal cost pricing ☐

B Risk bearing economies ☐

C Tax avoidance ☐

D Local multiplier effects ☐

6 **IKEA locates a large store in Argentina. This will cause:**

A A rise in the Argentinian peso and a positive multiplier effect ☐

B A depreciation in the Peso and a rise in aggregate demand ☐

C An increase in aggregate supply and a fall in aggregate demand ☐

D An increase in aggregate demand and a worsening in the balance
of payments ☐

7 **An increase in the percentage of GDP of a country made up by multinational companies is most likely to cause:**

A A rise in the budget surplus ☐

B An improvement in local technology ☐

C An increase in market competition ☐

D A fall in international competitiveness ☐

8 L'Oréal has large production facilities in Turkey. An increase in corporation tax and a rise in the HDI in Turkey is most likely to lead to:

   A   A fall in L'Oréal's profits ☐

   B   Capital flight from Turkey ☐

   C   Lower levels of productivity ☐

   D   increased use of transfer pricing ☐

9 Brazil is a key market for US consumer goods giants such as Proctor and Gamble. An imposition of an import tariff by Brazil on US consumer goods will most likely lead to:

   A   A fall in the price of US imports ☐

   B   Greater levels of US direct investment in Brazil relative to consumer goods exports ☐

   C   A rise in the US dollar –Brazilian Real exchange rate ☐

   D   An increase in Brazil`s current account deficit ☐

10 Governments may encourage outward investment by any of the following EXCEPT:

   A   Improving foreign language education ☐

   B   Putting restrictions on foreign remittances ☐

   C   Subsidising new technology ☐

   D   Reducing the level of protectionism ☐

Question 3

Multinational supply chains.

Match these terms to the correct definition in the table below:

Domestic supplier / Offshoring / Onshoring / Outsourcing / Inward FDI / Outward FDI / Exporting

How	Term used
The product is made abroad by a foreign company and sold at home	
The product is made at home by a local company and sold abroad	
The product is made at home by a foreign company and sold at home and abroad	
The product is made at home and sold at home	
The product was made abroad by a different company but has now been relocated at home	
The product is made abroad by the same company and sold at home	
The product is made abroad and sold abroad	

Question 4

a Explain the links between globalisation and multinational corporations

b Explain why multinational companies give rise to positive and negative externalities

c Explain why multinational companies such as Amazon and Unilever are able to dominate the market in a number of countries

d Explain why they are often able to produce at lower cost than smaller local firms

e Explain why foreign direct investment by a MNC may increase economic growth

Activity 6 | Protectionism

Follow the QR codes below to find out more about the latest trends in international trade patterns, free trade agreements and protectionism:

1	2	3
How are trade partnerships trading? From Our World In Data	**Tracking changing protectionist measures. From the International Institute of Sustainable Development. Look particularly at Figures 1, 2 and 3.**	**Homepage of the WTO's Regional Trade Partnerships database**

Question

Draw a demand and supply diagram representing a good for which the economy is an importer, and which shows:

a The impact of a new free trade agreement being signed

b The impact of a rise in temporary trade barriers

Activity 7 | Emerging economies

The CIA World Factbook gives comprehensive data about all economies. You can find it here:

Please use this data to examine two key groups of emerging economies:
- **The BRIC group:** The four large economies of Brazil, Russia, India and China are key players in world trade.
- **The MINT group:** The four fast-growing economies of Mexico, Indonesia, Nigeria and Turkey.

For each group: Select each country and review the section headed 'Economy' under the map of the country. Record the macroeonomic indicators for each country.

Activity 8 | Changing global supply chains

Question 1

Match each of these terms with one of the definitions given below:

Visit the Nike website, which allows you to trace how and where their different products are produced:

Select a couple of items, and note down the features of their supply chain.

Question 2

Read the article below, adapted from a 2019 Special Report in the Economist, considering how global supply chains are changing. Then answer the questions that follow.

OECD estimates suggest that 70% of all global trade now embeds "global value chains" i.e. the production of one good or service is spread across the world, with different components and value added in different countries. This globalisation of manufacturing processes occurred due to exploitation of lower labour costs overseas, access to raw materials, and the search for economies of scale. However, global trade slowed significantly between 2018 and 2019, driven by more localised differences such as European's data privacy laws, different approaches to environmental protection, and rising sentiments of protectionism (e.g. US President Trump's trade war with China). At the same time, companies such as Amazon and Alibaba aim to rapidly deliver endless choices to consumers, forcing modification of supply chains.

To some extent, these changes are being met by technological developments such as AI predictions of demand and robot-led warehouses and distribution centres. This is having the effect of shortening the supply chain, making them faster but potentially more complex. Half of the largest MNCs are considering making "major changes" to their supply chains, as they increasingly realise that lacking awareness of who/what is in their supply chain can cause significant disruption if there is a shock to the system, such as natural disaster or political events such as Brexit.

To reduce the impact, many firms are now ensuring that their supply chain is geographically closer to the end consumer. Some economists have argued that we are therefore experiencing "slowbalisation" or "regionalisation" rather than more globalisation. This may vary according to the industry in question. For example, electronics seem set to stay rooted in China for some time, but automobile production looks to be heading for regional 'hub and spoke' models.

a Think about the impact of the "rapid delivery" of items to consumers from companies such as Amazon and Alibaba. Complete the stakeholder grid below.

Stakeholder	Advantages	Disadvantages
End consumer		
Raw material producers		
Logistics / shipping companies		
End-manufacturer		

b Why might there be differences in the nature of global supply chains for different products?

c Note down as many ways as you can in which technology could continue to alter global supply chains. Be creative!

Question 3

The KOF Globalisation Index looks at 3 aspects of globalisation: political, economic and social and is constructed using the following components and weights:

Economic Globalisation	35%
Actual Flows	**50%**
Trade as a % of GDP	23%
FDI as a % of GDP	29%
Portfolio investment as a % of GDP	27%
Income payments to foreign nationals as a % of GDP	22%
Restrictions	**50%**
Hidden import barriers	20%
Mean tariff rate	30%
Taxes on int'l trade (as % of current revenue)	24%
Capital account restrictions	26%
Political Globalisation	**28%**
Embassies in country	34%
Membership of international organisations	34%
Participation in UN Security Council Missions	32%
Social Globalisation	**38%**
Data on personal contact	**24%**
Outgoing telephone traffic	31%
Transfers (% of GDP)	9%
International tourism	1%
Telephone average costs of call to the US	33%
Foreign population (% of total population)	26%

Table continues on next page

Social Globalisation *(continued)*	
Data on information flows	**24%**
Telephone mainlines per 1000 people	18%
Internet hosts per capita	15%
Internet users as % of population	18%
Cable TV per 1000 people	16%
Daily newspapers per 1000 people	16%
Radios per 1000 people	17%
Data on cultural proximity	**37%**
No of McDonald's restaurants per capita	100%

Note that weights may not sum to 100 because of rounding. The index ranges from 0 = not globalised to 100 = globalised.

Using the QR code on the right explore the interactive map/graphic that traces the extent to which different countries have engaged with globalisation since 1970 to the present day. Then compare and contrast the latest data with the data from 2018 – you can find the older data towards the bottom of the webpage, accessible via Zip files. Note your findings below:

THE UK ECONOMY NOW AND IN THE LAST 50 YEARS

Activity 1 | Definitions

Match each of these terms with one of the definitions given below:

a	Macroeconomic indicator	**b**	Real GDP	**c**	Inflation
d	Unemployment	**e**	Current account of the balance of payments	**f**	Base rate of interest
g	Inward FDI	**h**	Outward FDI	**i**	Privatisation
j	Nationalisation				

1	Sustained increase in the general price level for goods and services
2	Measures the difference between money and credit going in and out of an economy through exports, imports and income paid on assets both home and abroad
3	The rate of interest at which the Bank of England are prepared to make short-term loans available to the banking sector
4	A measurement of some aspect of the performance of an economy over time
5	Flows of capital from foreign multinationals (MNCs) to the domestic economy including takeovers and tangible investment in new factories and technology
6	Selling off a state-run industry to the private sector
7	The transfer of a major branch of industry or commerce from private to state ownership or control
8	Nominal GDP adjusted for price changes, expressed at constant prices
9	Flows of capital from domestic multinationals (MNCs) to overseas economies including takeovers and tangible investment in new factories and technology
10	When people would like to work and are available to start work but cannot find a job at the current wage rate

Activity 1 | The Historical Perspective – 1970 to 2018/9

Chart 1
GDP growth

Gross Domestic Product: Year on year growth

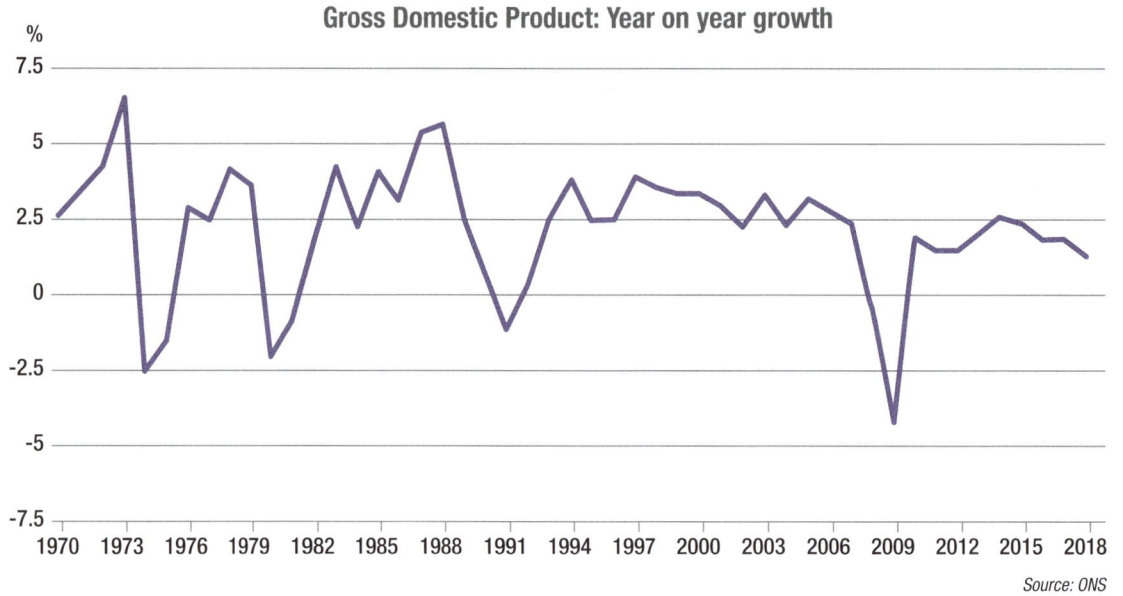

Source: ONS

Chart 2
Unemployment

UK Unemployment Rate (%)
ILO Measure

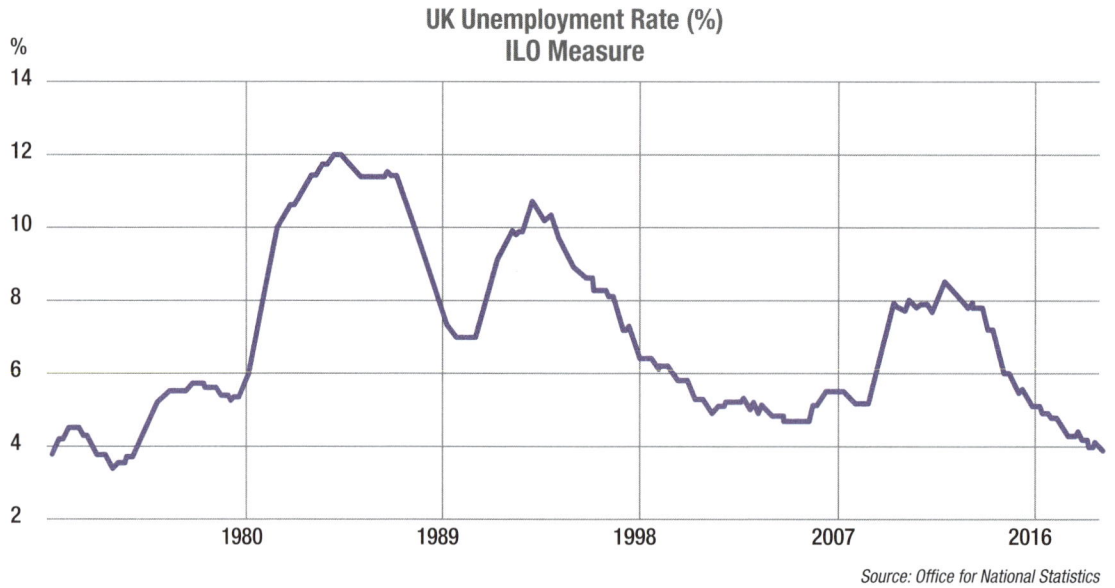

Source: Office for National Statistics

Chart 3
Retail Prices Index

RPI all Items: Percentage change over 12 months: Jan 1987=100

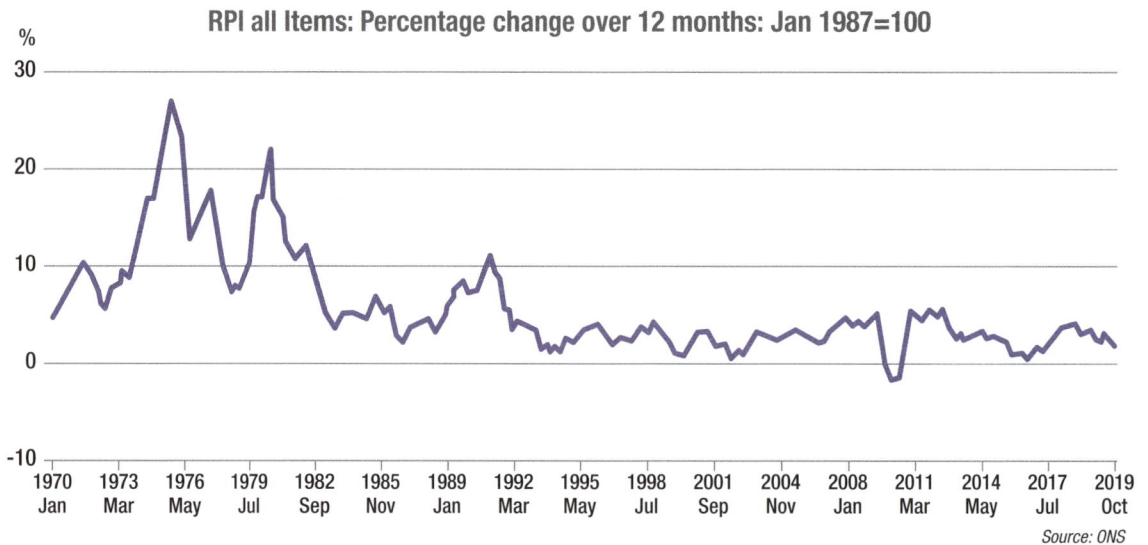

Source: ONS

The three charts on the previous page show the data for three of the UK's macroeconomic indicators from 1970 to 2018. Note that the third chart shows inflation measured by the Retail Prices Index (RPI) rather than Consumer Prices Index (CPI) – this is because there is no data for the CPI before 1988.

Question 1

Chart 1 showing the GDP growth rate demonstrates the Economic Cycle. Does every downturn in the cycle result in recession? Explain your answer.

Question 2

Do the unemployment rate and the inflation rate show the patterns that you would expect, given the corresponding rate of GDP growth?

Note any points at which the three indicators do not follow the pattern that you would expect.

Question 3

The list below gives a number of economic events which have all taken place between 1970 and 2018. Research each of these events to find out when they occurred, and with reference to the three charts above, note the apparent effect on GDP growth, unemployment and inflation of each event.

Economic event	When it occurred	Effect on GDP growth, unemployment and inflation
a OPEC oil embargo and oil price shocks		GDP: Unemployment: Inflation:
b The Winter of Discontent		GDP: Unemployment: Inflation:
c The Miners' Strike		GDP: Unemployment: Inflation:
d Election of Margaret Thatcher as Prime Minister		GDP: Unemployment: Inflation:
e Election of Tony Blair as Prime Minister		GDP: Unemployment: Inflation:
f House price crash		GDP: Unemployment: Inflation:

Economic event	When it occurred	Effect on GDP growth, unemployment and inflation
g UK joins the Exchange Rate Mechanism		GDP: Unemployment: Inflation:
h Black Wednesday		GDP: Unemployment: Inflation:
i The UK receives a loan from the IMF		GDP: Unemployment: Inflation:
j The 'Dot Com Bubble' bursts		GDP: Unemployment: Inflation:
k The financial markets 'Big Bang'		GDP: Unemployment: Inflation:
l The Credit Crunch		GDP: Unemployment: Inflation:
m UK government bail outs of Northern Rock, Lloyds TSB and RBS		GDP: Unemployment: Inflation:
n The UK's referendum decision to leave the EU		GDP: Unemployment: Inflation:
o The UK joins the EU		GDP: Unemployment: Inflation:
p The start of 60 consecutive quarters of positive economic growth		GDP: Unemployment: Inflation:
q Bank of England independence		GDP: Unemployment: Inflation:
r The UK government imposes a 'Three Day Week'		GDP: Unemployment: Inflation:

Activity 3 | Privatisation

All of the businesses listed in the table were privatised by the UK government, having been previously owned by the state.

Download Parliamentary Research Paper number 14/61, which was published on 20 November 2014 and is available online as a pdf file. Read that paper to find out when each business was privatised, and how much capital was raised for the government as a result of privatisation.

State owned business	When privatised	Capital raised
British Aerospace		
British Airways		
British Coal		
British Gas		
British Petroleum		
British Rail		
British Sugar Corporation		
British Telecom		
National Air Traffic Services		
Rolls Royce		
Thomas Cook		
Water industry		

Activity 4 | Focus on 2013 to 2022

This table on the following page gives some detailed data for a range of the UK's macroeconomic indicators from 2013 to 2022.

Study the data for each indicator, and add some comments about any patterns or anomalies you can identify, and any links that you can see between them.

Indicator	Data and comments									
	2013	2014	2015	2016	2017	2018	2019	2020	2021	2022
Real GDP (£trn)	1.67	1.72	1.76	1.79	1.82	1.85	2.26	2.05	2.20	tbc
Comment:										
Inflation (CPI) at end of year	2.6%	1.5%	0%	0.7%	2.7%	2.5%	1.3%	0.59%	5.39%	10.53%
Comment:										
Base Rate at end of year	0.5%	0.5%	0.5%	0.5%	0.5%	0.75%	0.75%	0.1%	0.25%	3.5%
Comment:										
Unemployment (LFS measure) at end of year	7.6%	6.2%	5.4%	4.9%	4.4%	4.1%	3.8%	4.7%	4.6%	3.7%
Comment:										
Part-time employment at end of year ('000s)	6 631	6 429	6 373	6 425	6 615	6 665	6 694	6 663	6 625	tbc
Comment:										

Indicator	Data and comments									
	2013	2014	2015	2016	2017	2018	2019	2020	2021	2022
Fiscal deficit as a percent of GDP	7.4%	5.8%	5.1%	4.3%	2.8%	2.7%	1.9%	15%	5.7%	7.8%

Comment:

Indicator										
Government debt as a percent of GDP	84.3%	85.7%	85.7%	85.4%	85.2%	84.6%	84.24%	94.9%	97.4%	99.5%

Comment:

Indicator										
£ : euro exchange rate at end of year	1.19	1.27	1.36	1.18	1.13	1.11	1.19	1.10	1.19	1.13

Comment:

Indicator										
£ : $ exchange rate at end of year	1.64	1.55	1.48	1.23	1.34	1.27	1.29	1.35	1.34	1.21

Comment:

Indicator										
Total exports as a percent of GDP	30.0%	28.5%	27.7%	28.4%	30.4%	30.0%	31.3%	29.2%	27.9%	tbc

Comment:

Indicator										
Total imports as a percent of GDP	31.2%	29.9%	29.0%	30.1%	31.6%	31.8%	32.9%	28.9%	28.7%	tbc

Comment:

Activity 5 | National Happiness

A rise in GDP suggests living standards are going up but may mask the true position.

Question 1

Suggest three reasons for this:

1

2

3

In 2010 the UK Prime Minister launched the *Measuring National Wellbeing programme* to 'start measuring our progress as a country, not just by how our economy is growing, but how our lives are improving; not just by our standard of living, but by our quality of life.' The Office for National Statistics (ONS) now compiles data covering 10 domains and 38 measures of wellbeing based on what people in the UK said actually mattered to them. As the ONS states, 'There are objective measures of wellbeing, like life expectancy and levels of unemployment, and also subjective measures – how people actually feel about progress, including overall satisfaction with life and levels of anxiety. It is important to have a mix because objective measures, such as actual crime levels, don't always reflect the way people feel, for example, their fear of crime – and the differences – can have important implications for policy.'

Question 2

Look at the latest 'dashboard of measures' on the ONS website. Summarise the state of wellbeing in the UK. Highlight the main factors affecting this.

Activity 6 | The jobs people do in the UK

Look at this information from the UK government on Employment by Occupation and Ethnicity and then use it to answer questions 1 and 2.

Question 1

a Which type of occupation has the highest proportion of workers in the UK? Is this the case for all ethnicities shown in the data?.

b Which type of occupation has the lowest proportion of workers in the UK? Is this the case for all ethnicities shown in the data?

Question 2

Which of the data formats shown (ie bar charts and data tables) is the easiest to understand and interpret? Why do you think this?

Now look at this information from the consulting firm McKinsey, which looks at why employees are leaving the workforce, and use it to answer questions 3 and 4.

Question 3

What does the report suggest about the impact of the Covid pandemic on UK labour market trends?

Question 4

What does the report suggest are the key reasons for these changes?

Finally, read the report for the House of Commons on the impact of the Covid pandemic on the UK labour market and use it to answer questions 5 and 6.

Question 5

Outline the trends in employment, unemployment and economic inactivity since the start of the pandemic

Question 6

Can you think of possible reasons that could explain the trends you have outlined in question 5?

UK GOVERNMENT FISCAL POLICY AND WELFARE BENEFITS

Activity 1 | Definitions

Question 1

Match each of these terms with one of the definitions given below:

a	Tax burden	b	Laffer curve	c	Austerity
d	Automatic stabilisers	e	Redistribution	f	Marginal rate of taxation
g	Personal allowance	h	State pension	i	Benefit cap
j	National insurance					

1	Economic policy aimed at reducing a government's deficit (or borrowing), achieved through increases in government revenues and/or a reduction in government spending or future spending commitments	
2	The rate of tax on the next unit (£1) of income earned	
3	The amount of income you can earn before you start paying income tax	
4	A limit on the total amount of benefit that most people aged 16 to 64 can get	
5	A measure of the total of tax revenues as a % of GDP	
6	A direct tax paid by those who are 16 or over and either an employee earning above £166 a week, or self-employed and making a profit of £6,365 or more a year	
7	Fiscal changes which occur as the economy moves through stages of the business cycle – e.g. a fall in tax revenues from the circular flow in a recession.	
8	A weekly benefit payment from the government to those over a certain age who have paid a minimum of 10 years' worth of National Insurance contributions	
9	A (supposed) relationship between economic activity and the rate of taxation which suggests there is an optimum tax rate which maximises total tax revenue	
10	Measures taken by government to transfer income from some individuals to others	

Activity 2 | Your tax payments

Question 1

Income taxes

Imagine that you have a job, earning £65,000. Use the government's website to find current tax rates, and calculate the amount of tax that you would be paying.

a Income tax

b **National Insurance Contributions** - You pay National Insurance contributions to qualify for certain state benefits and the State Pension. At the time of writing, anyone over 16 who earns over £166 in any week (even if they are not employed full-time) must pay National Insurance.

Question 2

Property taxes

Now imagine that you are buying a property which you will live in. You must pay Stamp Duty Land Tax (SDLT) if you buy a property or land over a certain price in England and Northern Ireland. You can calculate the current rates of Stamp Duty by following this QR code.

Find out how much stamp duty you would pay for each of the following properties, assuming that it will be your main residence. In each case, you should assume that the property will be freehold, not leasehold:

a A flat in Middlesborough for £100,000

b A semi-detached house in York for £250,000 which is your first home (you are a 'first-time buyer')

c A house in Bristol for £400,000

d A semi-detached house in Guildford for £750,000

e A detached house in Oxford for £1,000,000

f A house in Knutsford for £2,500,000

Question 3

Wealth taxes

You have inherited £50,000, and you decide to invest it by buying a second property which you will rent out (a 'buy-to-let' property). The property costs £250,000, so you will also need a mortgage of £200,000.

Find out:

a How much stamp duty you would pay for this additional property, using the government website Stamp Duty calculator used in Question 2 above but noting that this is an Additional residential property, and will not be replacing your main residence.

b Search the internet to find whether the mortgage interest rate for a 'buy-to-let' property is the same as the mortgage interest rate for a property that you buy to live in yourself.

You might decide to spend your inheritance on buying some shares on the London Stock Exchange instead.

c Find out how much stamp duty you would pay if you buy £50,000 worth of shares

Question 4

Inheritance tax

When someone dies, the total value of their money in savings, their property and other possessions must be calculated. This is known as their 'estate', and it may be liable for Inheritance Tax.

Find the current rate of inheritance tax, and the threshold at which the tax becomes payable, by following this QR code.

If you inherit an estate in which there is a house valued at £500,000 plus savings of £70,000, how much inheritance tax will you pay?

Activity 3 | Recent UK fiscal policy.

In the budget for financial year 2019-20, Total Managed Expenditure (TME) around £842 billion. The pie chart below shows TME broken down by main function.

Chart 1: Public sector spending 2019-20

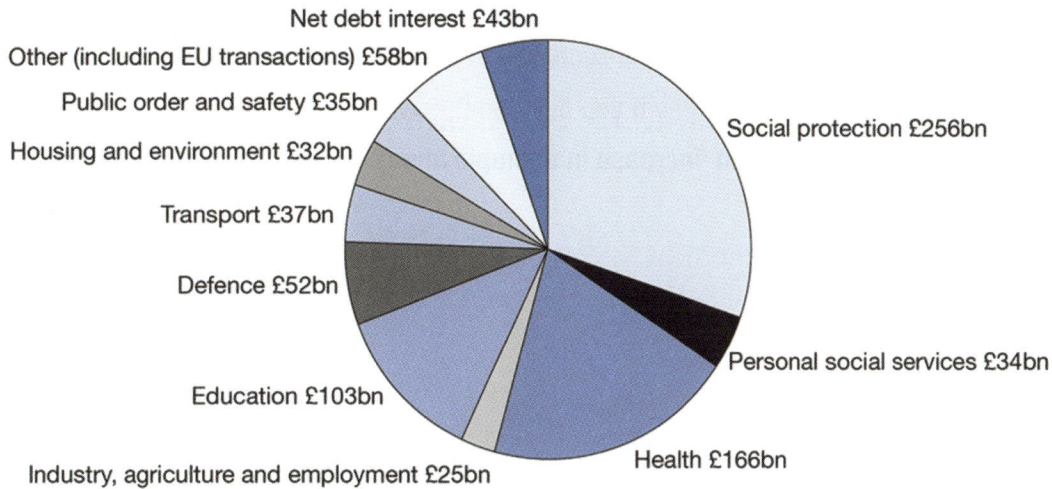

Net debt interest £43bn
Other (including EU transactions) £58bn
Public order and safety £35bn
Housing and environment £32bn
Transport £37bn
Defence £52bn
Education £103bn
Industry, agriculture and employment £25bn
Social protection £256bn
Personal social services £34bn
Health £166bn

N.B. social protection includes pensions and welfare.

To answer questions 1-4, use the latest pie chart on the ukpublicspending.co.uk website.

Question 1

Compare total government spending plans in the current year with the figures above.

a Has TME risen or fallen?

b What are the most significant changes to budgeted spending on the main functions shown in the pie chart?

Question 2

What percentage of the budget does the UK government now spend on social protection?

Question 3

Explain why an 'ageing population' and an 'increase in unemployment' would be a major concern for any government.

Question 4

Net Debt interest in 2019-20 was expected to be £43bn. Explain why this figure was higher than the budgeted Net Debt Interest figure of £39bn in 2016-17.

In the budget for financial year 2019-20, public sector current receipts were £810 billion. Chart 2 below shows the different sources of government revenue.

Chart 2: Public sector current receipts 2019-20

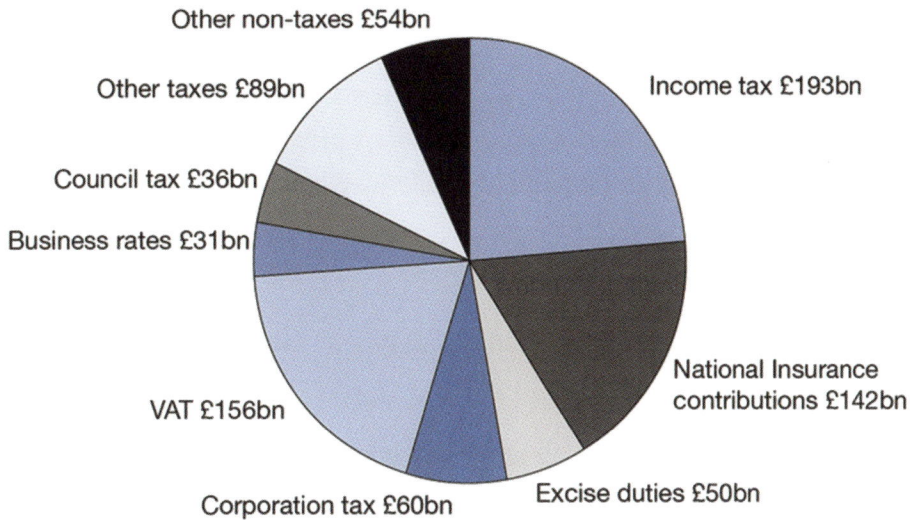

Other taxes includes capital taxes, stamp duties, vehicle excise duties and other smaller tax receipts. Other non-taxes includes interest and dividends, gross operating surplus and other smaller non-tax receipts.

To answer questions 5-8, use the latest pie chart on the ukpublicrevenue.co.uk website.

Question 5

Compare total expected tax receipts in the current year with the figures for 2019-20 above.

a Has the figure for total expected tax receipts risen or fallen?

b Why is that – what are the most significant changes to expected receipts from the different taxes shown in the pie chart?

Question 6

Explain the difference between 'tax avoidance' and 'tax evasion', and why they are a concern for any government.

Question 7

Corporation tax rates changed in April 2023. Small businesses, with profits of under £50 000 per year, will continue to pay corporation tax at a rate of 19%. However, larger businesses with profits of over £250 000, will now pay corporation tax at a higher rate of 25%. Explain how these changes in tax could affect the government's receipts from corporation tax.

Question 8

National Insurance is paid by both employers and employees. Find the current rates for national insurance payments for each of those parties.

Activity 4 | Benefits and the Welfare State

Jobseekers Allowance (JSA) is the financial welfare benefit available to people who are unemployed. However, not everyone qualifies to claim it – this is one of the reasons that the Claimant Count measure of unemployment is lower than the Labour Force Survey measure.

Question 1

Visit the government's website about Jobseekers Allowance at: https://www.gov.uk/jobseekers-allowance, and find at least 3 reasons why someone may not be able to claim JSA.

In this part of the website https://www.gov.uk/disability-premiums, find out when someone might be able to claim benefits because of their own disability, or https://www.gov.uk/carers-allowance because they are caring for someone else.

The government also makes some extra payments available to those who are working, but are on a low income.

Question 2

Find out the circumstances that would allow a worker to claim Income Support.

Question 3

Child Benefit is a universal benefit, paid to everyone who has a child.

Visit the government's website at https://www.gov.uk/child-benefit, and find out:

a When Child Benefit is paid and who receives it

b How Child Benefit is treated for those earning a higher income

Question 4

Why does the government choose to redistribute income via the benefits you have examined?

DIFFERENT ECONOMIC SYSTEMS

Activity 1 | Definitions

Question 1

Match each of these terms with one of the definitions given below:

a Command economy		**b** State intervention		**c** Progressive taxation	
d Free market		**e** Public goods		**f** Public sector	
g Price mechanism		**h** Function of money		**i** Transition economy	
j Property rights					

1	When consumption of the good by one person does not reduce the amount available for consumption by another person, and it is not possible to provide a good or service to one person without it being available for others to enjoy
2	When there is a medium of exchange, a store of value, a unit of account and a standard of deferred payment
3	When resources that are directly, or indirectly, used in an exchange have a specific or identifiable owner
4	When action taken by government seeks to change the decisions made by individuals, groups and organisations about social and economic matters
5	When central government, local government and public corporations take a role in providing goods and services
6	When the government owns and allocates scarce resources and sets production targets and growth rates
7	When economies are involved in a process of moving from a centrally planned economy to a mixed or free market economy
8	When markets allocate resources through the price mechanism
9	When there is a means by which decisions of consumers and businesses interact to determine the allocation of resources
10	When the marginal rate of tax rises as income rises

Activity 2 | Features of economic systems

The table below gives the three categories of economic system – free market, command and mixed economies. Complete columns 2 and 3 of the table by matching the advantages and disadvantages of each economic system, from the lists which are also given below.

	Advantages	Disadvantages
Free market economy		
Command economy		
Mixed economy		

List of advantages and disadvantages

A	Resources are allocated for the common good	B	Lack of public goods
C	Competitive prices for consumers	D	Can be difficult to determine how much governments should intervene
E	Businesses are free to decide what to produce, but there are government regulations to reduce monopoly power	F	High bureaucratic costs can lead to wasteful spending
G	Efficient allocation of scarce resources	H	The existing government 'safety net' may still allow inequality
I	Can be faster to build major infrastructure projects	J	Profit motive may lead firms to cut corners
K	The economy is largely driven by private investment and enterprise, but government can intervene to reduce fluctuations in the economic cycle	L	Discretionary fiscal policy may create alternative problems such as a high level of government borrowing
M	Tends to lead to faster GDP growth	N	Absence of incentives for workers and businesses
O	Low levels of inequality and unemployment	P	Inaccuracy in setting suitable prices for goods and services
Q	People can enjoy the financial rewards of hard work and entrepreneurship while there is a 'safety net' of welfare provision	R	Some of the labour force may be unable to find work

Activity 3 | The role of government in different economies

Access online the CIA World Factbook at:
https://www.cia.gov/the-world-factbook/

For each of the countries in the table below, read the 'Economy' section provided by the World Factbook which can be found in the drop-down menus below the map of the country, to find the following data:

a GDP per capita at PPP

b GDP composition - Government Consumption as a percentage of GDP

c Unemployment rate

d Distribution of family income – GINI index

e Taxes and other revenues as a percentage of GDP

f Public debt as a percentage of GDP

g Market value of publicly traded shares (note whether this data is not given)

h Stock of direct foreign investment at home

i Stock of direct foreign investment abroad

You can add a country of your own choice.

After completing your research, decide whether you can identify which of these economies best fits the description of a free market economy, a command economy and a mixed economy.

Country	GDP per capita	Govt consumption	Unemployment	Gini	Tax % of GDP	Public debt % of GDP	Value of shares	FDI at home	FDI abroad
UK									
Singapore									
Cuba									
Norway									
China									
Switzerland									
Your choice									

Activity 4 | Government spending on public services

The OECD website compares the amount of government spending on various public services as a percentage of GDP.

For each of the countries listed in Activity 3 above, find the following:

a The percentage of government spending on health care as a percentage of GDP

b On education

c A report produced by the Global Change Data Lab at the University of Oxford compares public spending in most countries of the world (although, unfortunately, excluding Cuba).

Scan this report to make comparisons between the countries you are investigating. Note that most of the charts are interactive, and you can choose which countries you wish to investigate.

Activity 5 | Indexing Economic Freedom

The Fraser Institute is a Canadian economic think tank, whose stated mission is to "improve the quality of life for Canadians, their families, and future generations by studying, measuring, and broadly communicating the effects of government policies, entrepreneurship, and choice on their well-being." Their economic stance is based on the free-market, and they produce an annual report on the Economic Freedom of the World.

The Fraser Institute 2022 report – PDF format.

The Fraser Institute 2020 interactive map.

The Heritage Foundation is a similar think tank in the US, with a stated purpose to "formulate and promote conservative public policies based on the principles of free enterprise, limited government, individual freedom, traditional American values, and a strong national defense."

The Heritage Foundation also produces an index and data on Economic Freedom. The interactive 2022 version can be found by following the QR code to the right.

Task 1

Read the introductions to these two reports, and list the broad areas in which each of them seeks to measure Economic Freedom.

Task 2

In both indexes in 2019/2020, Hong Kong was ranked as the economy with the greatest economic freedom. However it is notable that in 2019 there were strong protests in Hong Kong about the role of China and potential limits to Hong Kong's economic freedom.

Research news websites such as the BBC or other independent sources, to discover the current situation in Hong Kong, and make a judgement about whether economic freedom is becoming more limited.

Task 3

In 2019, the founder of the Heritage Foundation (Edwin Feulner), commented on the improvement in the US's ranking to 12th in the index. He said that this was due to "significant improvements in scores for tax burden and government integrity" and in spite of "new protectionist policies that have raised tariffs and disrupted established manufacturing supply chains (that) are just beginning to affect consumer prices and investment decisions". In the 2022 rankings, the US was 25th.

Research news websites such as the BBC or other independent sources, to discover the current situation concerning tax burdens and also protectionist policies in the US, and make a judgment about whether economic freedom is becoming more limited.

TRADE BLOCS

Activity 1 | Definitions

Question 1

Match each of these terms with one of the definitions given below:

a	Free trade	b	Protectionism	c	Trade creation
d	Trade liberalisation	e	Trade diversion	f	Comparative advantage
g	Bi-lateral trade agreement	h	Regional trade agreement	i	The WTO
j	The UN				

1	The movement from a higher cost source of output to a lower cost source of supply as a result of joining a trade agreement
2	A switch from a lower-cost foreign source/supplier outside of a customs union towards a higher-cost supplier located inside the customs union
3	An organisation which polices free trade agreements, and decides on trade disputes between countries. It arranges trade negotiations to liberalize trade for member countries by mutually agreed reductions in tariffs & quotas and opening domestic markets up to foreign competition
4	When a country can benefit from specialising in and exporting the product(s) for which it has the lowest opportunity cost of supply
5	An organisation responsible for maintaining international peace and security, developing friendly relations among nations, achieving international cooperation, and being a centre for harmonising the actions of nations
6	When there are no tariffs or taxes or quotas on goods and/or services from one country entering another
7	Reductions in import tariffs and non-tariff barriers to enhance trade between one or more countries
8	An agreement to lower import tariffs and other trade barriers between countries in a certain region
9	An agreement to lower import tariffs and other trade barriers between two countries – for example between South Korea and Australia
10	Tariff and non-tariff restrictions on imports to protect domestic producers

Activity 2 | What is a Trade Bloc?

Trade blocs are groups of countries in specific regions that manage and promote trade activities. Trade blocs lead to trade liberalisation (the freeing of trade from protectionist measures) and trade creation between members, since they are treated favourably in comparison to non-members.

Carry out some research to find out about the differences between different types of trade agreements, which are listed across the top of the table below. **www.tutor2u.net** might be a good place to start your research!

On the table, tick each of the features of a trade agreement listed at the left hand side of the table, which apply to each of the different types of agreement listed along the top of the table.

	Preferential trade area	Free trade area	Customs union	Common market	Economic union	Full integration
Lower barriers						
Uniform economic policies						
Common external barriers						
Entities behave as one unit						
Free flow of resources						
Eliminate barriers						

Activity 3 | The Transatlantic Trade and Investment Programme

The Transatlantic Trade and Investment Programme (TTIP) was the name of a potential free-trade agreement between the EU and the US. Negotiations were halted after the election of Donald Trump as US President, and although there have been attempts to re-start, at the time of writing these have failed.

> **Read this item from the Tutor2u website and answer the following questions:**

Question 1

What non-tariff barriers did the TTIP propose?

Question 2

Draw a tariff diagram to show why big businesses might hope to benefit from a free trade deal such as TTIP.

Question 3

Why were opponents such as Trade Unions and the environmental movement oppose TTIP?

Activity 4 | NAFTA and USMCA

Question 1

Find out what both of these trade bloc titles stand for, which countries they involve, and how they relate to each other.

Question 2

This article from CNN lists 6 differences between NAFTA and USMCA:

Summarise these differences:

Activity 5 | Other trade blocs

Use research to find out which countries are included in each of the following trade blocs:

ASEAN

Read this article about the economic diversity of the members of ASEAN and its economic community:

Mercosur

Read this article about a trade agreement between the EU and Mercosur:

APEC
Read this article about APEC:

Comesa
Read this article about attempts to establish a large EU-style free trade area in Africa:

INTERNATIONAL MACROECONOMIC BODIES

Your task is to research at least one of these international bodies, and prepare either:

a a 6-slide PowerPoint presentation

b a factsheet

which you could use to teach the rest of your class about them. You should include one slide/box on your factsheet on each of the following:

1 When they were formed and who by

2 Their purpose

3 Who the 'members' are

4 Recent news about them

5 Where possible, examples of their international operations – with advantages and disadvantages

6 Evaluate their effectiveness in achieving their purpose

NOTES